EXCITING
malaysia
a visual journey

Welcome to Malaysia, an
exotic land where
East meets West.

PERIPLUS

1 Malacca

2 Malacca

EXCITING
malaysia
a visual journey

To the visitor, Malaysia is a riot of colours and impressions, smells and noises, tastes and experiences. A land of natural wonders and ancient traditions, it stretches from the rugged mountainous rainforests of Sabah and Sarawak in Borneo to peaceful undulating plantations, picture-perfect villages and the pristine sandy beaches that are the trademark of the Peninsula's East Coast.

Yet Malaysia is also a dynamic modern nation proud of its busy cities full of skyscrapers, sophisticated factories, five-star hotels and excellent restaurants.

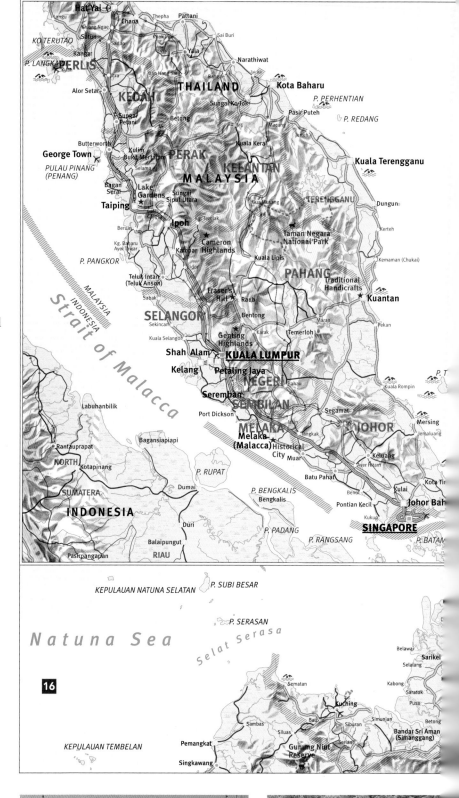

15 Sarawak: Kuching

14 Sarawak

Kuala Lumpur

4 Taman Negara National Park

5 Cameron Highlands

6 Terengganu

7 Kelantan

8 Perak

9 Penang

MALAYSIA

Sabah

12 Sabah

11 Langkawi

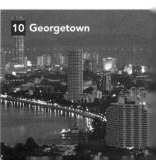

10 Georgetown

Malaysians are famous for their hospitality and *selamat datang* means welcome in *Bahasa Malaysia*, the national language of Malaysia.

Far right: The Moorish-inspired Sultan Abdul Samad building, once the power base of British rule, overlooks Merdeka ('Independence') Square, where Malaysia first celebrated its freedom from colonial rule.

Right: Independence Day (*Hari Merdeka*) is being celebrated by this Malay girl bearing a traditional coconut tree-inspired decoration.

MALAYSIA HAS PERFECTED the art of hospitality over a long, long time. Thanks to Peninsular Malaysia's position along the ancient sea trading routes of India, the Middle East and China, some of the earliest travellers to the country were merchants who sold exotic spices in return for rainforest products. We can only imagine what these visitors from foreign lands thought and felt as they glimpsed the uninterrupted white beaches which fringe Malaysia's coasts or as they journeyed inland through the world's oldest tropical rainforests. These natural wonders remain and continue to welcome visitors to modern-day Malaysia.

atang!

MUSEUM

CHRIST CHURCH MELAKA

T RADE HAS PLAYED a vital role in the development of Malaysia. Trade helped to build the great Malay empires of the 15th century and brought visitors such as the Indians, Arabs and Chinese. By the 16th century the great European trading empires were attracted by 'Malaya' (as it was known during colonial times) and first the Portuguese, then the Dutch (see left) and finally the British exerted control over the country. Finally, in 1957, Malaya gained independence and Malaysia, incorporating Sabah and Sarawak, came into being in 1963. Export of Malaysia's abundant natural resources, including tin, timber, rubber and petroleum, has fuelled the country's economic development. Industrialisation has enabled the country to grow from the security of a solid manufacturing base to intensive investment in new industries and digital technology. Malaysia's economic story is so successful that the country is acknowledged as one of the nations at the forefront of ASEAN (Association of Southeast-Asian Nations) and a powerful 'Tiger Nation'.

Left: The old Town Square in Malacca, popular with camera-happy tourists and bridal couples, is a remnant of the 18th century when the whole city was rebuilt in the image of a Dutch trading town. **Above:** Traditional bamboo blinds, called *chik*, provide welcome shade on a hot day.

Clockwise from top: Lush paddy fields contrast with the subdued, mist-curtained mountains of Sabah's West Coast; fine white sand and crystal-clear waters are the trademarks of Langkawi; charming colonial buildings dot the hill station of the Cameron Highlands.

tHE MULTIPLE CULTURES brought to Malaysia via trade and colonisation have contributed to the potpourri of influences that make up the modern nation: multi-ethnic, multi-lingual, multi-faith, urban and rural, East and West, old and new, natural and man-made. But despite rapid change Malaysians have held on to their traditions. Malaysia is a country where the mysticism of Chinese *feng shui* (the art of harmonious living) and Islamic religious values sit alongside a rapidly evolving modern society. Healers and fortune tellers are consulted despite the widespread availability of Western medicine. This adherance to tradition and acceptance of change has led, inevitably, to an unusual and stimulating landscape where internationally-hailed architecture looms over rickety stalls. Colonial hill stations, whose staff maintain the stately British tradition of High Tea, can still be found amid the big business of vast tea plantations. Sprawling traditional *kampungs* (villages) are situated next to pristine world-class golf courses. The list goes on. The contrasts which can be witnessed daily in Malaysia are almost bewildering, rarely forgettable and always fascinating.

people

A melting pot of origins, Malaysia's 22 million people boast a complex culture which has been influenced and enriched by many religious beliefs, cuisines and world views.

Opposite: The three main races of Malaysia – the Malays, Chinese and Indians. **Opposite, inset:** A friendly Malaysian welcome. **This page, clockwise from top:** Cosmopolitan, Western-influenced Malaysian urbanites; Islam is the dominant influence in the life of most Malays; the Chinese live mainly in the cities; the Sikh Malaysians in this *Bhangra* dance band preserve their traditions.

Multi-racialism has been a fact of life for Malaysia's 22 million people since Malacca's early trading days (15th century). Although the main races are the Malays, Chinese, Indians and the indigenous peoples of Sabah and Sarawak, intermarriage and immigration have resulted in the creation of a myriad of minor ethnic groups. Among them are the *Baba-Nonyas* (Malay culture-influenced Chinese); the *Chittys* (Malay culture-influenced Indians); *Mamaks* (Indian Muslims); and Eurasians (including descendants of the Portuguese and British). Then there are the indigenous people of Peninsular Malaysia, the *Orang Asli* (meaning 'original people'), who still live forest-bound lives.

Clockwise from top: This *Tok Dalang* (puppet master) tells ancient tales with his shadow plays; Malay boys in Kedah take a break from football; a Penan from Sarawak poses in his rainforest home; Indian shop-owners relax on their goods-cluttered 'five-foot way' (pavement).

Clockwise from top: A *Nonya* (woman of mixed Chinese and Malay heritage) oversees the sale of joss-sticks and sacred paper in the Buddhist Snake Temple in Penang; Kelantanese women rule market trading; these Chinese shop-owners in Johor Bahru sell different types of rice.

Clockwise from top: Friday prayers see Muslim men everywhere congregate in mosques and small meeting places in villages, called *surau*; Islam permeates every aspect of Malay life; the call to prayer resounds five times a day from the majestic Masjid Ubudiah Mosque in Perak's royal capital, Kuala Kangsar.

religion

Freedom of worship in this land of many faiths makes for a spiritually-rich people.

i SLAMIC MOSQUES, BUDDHIST temples and Hindu shrines can often be found along the same road in any town or village in Malaysia. From another corner might come the ringing of a bell in a Sikh temple, from yet another, the strains of a Catholic hymn. Meanwhile in rainforests, the *Orang Asli* practise animistic rites. Religious tolerance allows Malaysians to pray to their own gods, whoever they may be, even though Islam is the official religion. Throughout the year, people's lives are coloured with the noise, sights and excitement of numerous religious celebrations.

Clockwise from top: Stone deities in Hindu temples are the work of master carvers from India; worshippers throng Kuala Lumpur's Batu Caves during Thaipusam, the Hindu festival of penance; a bride, resplendent in traditional red sari, is blessed at her wedding; the century-old Hindu shrine at the Batu Caves attracts devotees from all over Malaysia.

Clockwise from top (far left): The smoke from joss sticks is believed to carry the prayers of Buddhist devotees up to heaven; this temple in Penang honours Kuan Yin, the Goddess of Mercy and the favourite deity of the Malaysian Chinese; the elaborate Khoo Kongsi clanhouse has housed ancestral tablets of Chinese bearing the Khoo name since 1840.

**The 740 kilometres of Peninsular Malaysia and the
vast Borneo states of Sarawak and Sabah boast a
unique environmental heritage.**

nature

Opposite: Orangutans roam the rainforests and can be observed at special sanctuaries in Sabah and Sarawak.
Clockwise from right: The National Park of Taman Negara has a popular canopy walkway slung high in the treetops; the entrance to one of Mulu National Park's magnificent caves; deliciously refreshing waterfalls dot the rainforests; visitors can go on short or extensive rainforest treks.

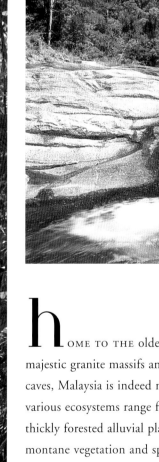

h OME TO THE oldest rainforests on earth, majestic granite massifs and astounding ancient caves, Malaysia is indeed nature's treasuretrove. Its various ecosystems range from muddy mangroves to thickly forested alluvial plains, scraggly hillside montane vegetation and spongy peat swamps. Malaysia harbours rare and endangered animals, birds and plants, some of which are exclusive to Malaysia. Many areas of the country have been gazetted as parks and sanctuaries affording the tourist, researcher and nature-lover access to a precious, globally diminishing resource.

kuala lu

mpur

Clockwise from top: Moorish influence is evident in the architecture of the capital's Central Railway Station; lights transform the city at night; a skybridge links the world's tallest buildings, the 452 m glass-and-steel Petronas Twin Towers.

Known as KL, Malaysia's capital city is the heartbeat of the nation's political, economic and financial life. Kuala Lumpur's impressive Twin Towers (left) are an apt embodiment of the country's soaring aspirations.

Clockwise from top: The country's most expensive real estate is located at the grid roads immediately south of Jalan Ampang, known to locals as 'The Golden Triangle'; the Gombak River winds calmly through the ever-changing cityscape; the new Light Rail System (LRT) is a panacea to the city's gridlocked traffic woes; the Merdeka Day parade through the city's historic centre is a colourful annual event.

Opposite: Modern malls such as Lot 10 on Bukit Bintang offer the discerning shopper an entire range of products from international brands to quality local goods.

Clockwise from top: Open-air food stalls tempt passersby with delicious smells; youngsters enjoy a weekend in the park; locals throng the night markets (called *pasar malam*) which sell everything from vegetables to compact discs and clothes; trendy urban girls; satay, the spicy Asian barbequed meat, is a popular snack.
Opposite: Red lanterns bedeck Chinatown's Petaling Street during Chinese New Year.

f ROM ITS HUMBLE beginnings as a tin-mining town at the muddy confluence of the rivers Klang and Gombak, Kuala Lumpur has evolved into a vibrant, cosmopolitan city. Monuments erected at the advent of Malaysia's independence are now dwarfed by the exposed steel and concrete stanchions of numerous new buildings under construction. Yet this bustling urban home to 1.5 million citizens is not without its interesting nooks and crannies, streetlife and traditional hawker (stall) food.

Clockwise from top: The funicular railway chugs up Penang Hill; the influence of Thailand and Myanmar can be seen in Penang's Buddhist temples; the island claims its fame from its hawker fare such as spicy Penang *laksa* (noodles, fishcakes and prawns in spicy coconut soup). **Opposite:** Penang's 10,000 Buddhas Precious Pagoda is the crowning glory of Malaysia's biggest Buddhist temple complex, Kek Lok Si.

penang
and
langkawi

THE NORTHERN ISLES of Penang, Pearl of the Orient, and Langkawi, Island of Legends, entice visitors time and again to their shores. While Penang has grown more urban as a result of its economic success – it is Malaysia's Silicon Valley – it has retained a unique character. Century-old architecture and a hotch-potch of streets and fascinating alleys remain at the heart of Penang's centre. A Heritage Trail snakes through colonial buildings, such as St George's Anglican church (built in 1817) and the E & O Hotel (built in 1884), colourful Chinese clanhouses, temples and busy street bazaars. Five-star hotels line Batu Feringghi beach while small fishing villages dot the island's outer reaches.

Clockwise from top: Penang's Georgetown, featuring the landmark Komtar Tower (background); trishaws still ply the narrow streets of Penang; Langkawi's seven-tier Telaga Tujuh waterfall provides a cool respite from the heat; fabulous views and clear, calm waters are Langkawi's offerings; one of Penang's fine sandy beaches, Batu Feringghi.

Opposite: Langkawi boasts some of the country's most beautiful hotels. Ranging from the subtly luxurious to boutique hotels and sprawling complexes of budget chalets, architectural inspiration has been drawn from Bali, Japan and Europe as well as traditional Malay houses.

t HE INHABITANTS OF Langkawi are pleased that Princess Mahsuri, who cursed the island as she lay dying (after a false accusation of adultery), no longer rules their island. Princess Mahsuri declared that her curse would survive seven generations and, since the curse was finally exhausted at the beginning of the 1990s, Langkawi has been a prosperous place. No one knows if the reason for Langkawi's popularity is the lifting of the curse or simply the discovery of the island by the international tourist trade, but one thing is certain: the island of Langkawi and its surrounding 98 islands offer the visitor some of the most beautiful beaches, clearest waters and most luxurious hotels in the world.

historic
malacca

Clockwise from top: The Porta de Santiago is the only surviving gateway of the Portuguese-built fort A Famosa; the women in this family on Jalan Kota wear *baju kurung*, traditional Malay dress; Malacca is home to a large *Peranakan* (which means 'born here') Chinese community, and these tiny shoes are a reminder of the days when bound feet were considered a mark of beauty; Portuguese descendents still retain their bond with the sea; in ancient times, bullock carts transported the wealthy.

THE MODERN HISTORY of Peninsular Malaysia began in 1400 in Malacca, an important port which was a centre of both East-West trade and magnificent Malay empires. In 1511, a series of colonisations began, starting with the Portuguese and then (in 1641) the Dutch. In 1824 Malacca came under British rule and along with Penang and Singapore formed part of the Straits Settlements. Today, the architecture of central Malacca remains unchanged since British rule and the cultures of the Straits-born Chinese (known as *Peranakan*), Portuguese Eurasians and Chitty Indians are evident in the city's architecture, religion and *Nonya* cuisine.

Clockwise from top: The Sri Poyyatha Vinayagar Moorthi Temple was one of the country's first Hindu temples; 17th century Chinese temples dot the Jonkers Street area; trishaws, an old-fashioned means of transport, survive as tourist attractions; an example of the imaginative decoration to be found on trishaws; Portuguese descendents show off their cultural heritage.

Opposite page: Christ Church serves as testament to Dutch architectural wizardry, boasting joint-less ceiling beams and handmade pews.

charming
east coast

Opposite: Perfect blue skies reflect off the clear waters of the East Coast islands.

a WHITE SANDY beach runs all the way south from the Thai border through the Malaysian states of Kelantan, Terengganu and Pahang. This is the Peninsula's East Coast and life here is leisurely, relying on a sea-bound existence and traditional fishing methods. Malaysia's East Coast is less populated than the West Coast and, due to its exposure to different cultural influences, such as Thai, has a unique character. However, the recent discovery of oil has brought modernisation, and tourism has gained a foothold in resorts such as Cherating and on the coral-rich isles off the mainland.

Clockwise from top: Buying the day's supply of fresh fish from the ocean; tourist boats sit alongside fishing vessels in numerous East Coast ports (which act as jumping-off points to holiday isles); fruit galore colours this outdoor market in Kuala Terengganu.

Above: From fresh produce to batik, spices and aromatic local cakes, Kota Bharu's open-air Central Market, *Pasar Besar*, is a riotous cornucopia. **Right:** Marang holds the distinction of being one of the most picturesque villages on the East Coast.

O WHERE IS Malay culture more predominant than in Kelantan. The various *kampungs* or villages around the state capital, Kota Bharu, are arts centres where silversmiths hammer out fine silverware; wax-and-paint batik pieces are created; gold-threaded *songket* material woven and giant *wau bulan* kites strung together. East of the city *bangau* fishing boats, featuring mythological figures, are elaborately carved and painted. Traditional wood-carving adorns palaces, museums and even homes. Cultural festivals, which feature top-spinning and kite-flying competitions, are popular among locals and tourists alike.

Clockwise from top: Malay designs adorn traditional vessels; massive *wau bulan* or 'moon kites' are as intricately decorated as *bangau* boats; traditional top-spinning competitions are crowd-pullers; fishing boats are lovingly painted.

sabah
and
sarawak

Top: Kota Kinabalu's Tanjung Aru Beach. **Above:** One of Sabah's endangered green-back turtles.

Majestic mountains, age-old jungles, and ancient traditions contribute to the fascinations of East Malaysia.

Clockwise from top: Mount Kinabalu, Southeast Asia's highest peak, is sacred to the Kadazan people who live in the area surrounding the mountain; *Bobohizan*, priests and priestesses, bless the Gawai Harvest Festival, Sabah; children crossing a suspension bridge near Kota Belud; Bajau tradition is preserved in dance.

Land of the orangutan and the hornbill, the natural splendour of Sabah and Sarawak is undisputed. Thousands of kilometres of rivers spring from the highlands, wind through rainforests, and end in river basins. The indigenous peoples have lived along the riverbanks since ancient times, using the river for water, transport and food and the forests for food and shelter. Today, modern cities have sprung up along the coast. Sabah's protected natural areas offer unique sights to the tourist. The Kinabalu National Park has the world's largest collection of wild orchids; the Turtle Islands Sanctuary is a vital turtle breeding ground; the Kinabatangan Basin is a rare refuge for proboscis monkeys; and the Tunku Abdul Rahman Marine Park is a coral reef sanctuary.

Clockwise from top: A taste of indigenous culture can be found at the Sarawak Cultural Village in Kuching; indigenous Sarawakian culture, such as that of the Iban, is very much alive in every aspect including dress (right) and dance (left).

Clockwise from top:
Overlooking the Sungei Sarawak, Fort Margherita (built in 1879) is one of 20 forts constructed on the orders of Charles Brooke (1829–1917), the English ruler of Sarawak, to control the inhabitants of the area. Fort Margherita is now a Police Museum; the rain-sculpted stone jungle known as the Pinnacles, Mulu; knick-knacks, handicrafts and antiques abound in Kuching's bazaar; the Sarawak Museum's collection of artefacts from Borneo is among Southeast Asia's finest.

THE LARGEST STATE in Malaysia, Sarawak has emerged from its violent pirating and head-hunting past into a prosperous present fuelled by commerce, petroleum products, timber and pepper. Sarawak's extraordinary cultural and natural diversity means that the visitor can stay at a traditional longhouse, observe prehistoric rites at the Gawai Harvest Festival, or make a trip to the Sarawak Chamber, a cave which is the world's largest single enclosed space, measuring 600 metres in length, 450 metres in width and 100 metres in height.

wonders of the sea

Malaysia's colourful marine kingdom stretches from the Straits of Malacca to the South China Sea.

M ALAYSIA'S SHALLOW TROPICAL waters nurture some of the world's most biodiverse coral reefs. From delicate anemones to large clumps of staghorn corals, Malaysian reefs are home to a staggering range of marine life. The sandy bottom provides a refuge for rare shells and tiny gobies, while the top of the coral is graced with groups of pretty basslets. At the more dramatic end of the marine-life scale the grouper and the ancient sea turtle, symbol of Tourism Malaysia, entertain snorkellers with their character and grace.

Opposite: A sport diver is treated to an encounter with a shoal of butterfly fish.

Clockwise from top: an angelfish from the waters of Sabah; these moray eels peep out from their home; a school of sleek barracudas looks for prey; the tiny nudibranch feeds on algae and sponges; a hawkfish perches on coral.

Clockwise from left: These lovely corals grow on a calcium carbonate skeleton built out of the remains of previous generations of aquatic life; this lionfish roams the reef at night; the timid yellow trumpetfish could be mistaken for a drifting stick; basslets forage for food amidst staghorn coral.

bECAUSE OF AN increased awareness of the importance of marine ecosystems, 38 of Malaysia's precious coral reefs have been protected as marine parks. The best reefs are located in the crystal-clear waters off islands such as Redang and Perhentian (Terengganu). Sipadan, in Sabah, is recognised as one of the finest dive sites in the world. Malaysia's reef life is characterised by vivid colours and abundant life, much of which is endemic to specific sites – making diving and snorkelling in Malaysian waters a truly unique experience.

Left: Trishaws are still used in some parts of Malaysia.

Published by Periplus Editions (HK) Ltd

ISBN 978-962-593-755-7

Distributors:
Asia Pacific
Berkeley Books Pte Ltd
61 Tai Seng Avenue, #02-12, Singapore 534167
Tel: (65) 6280 1330; Fax: (65) 6280 6290
Email: inquiries@periplus.com.sg
www. periplus.com

North America, Latin America & Europe
Tuttle Publishing
364 Innovation Drive
North Clarendon, VT 05759-9436 USA
Tel: 1 (802) 773-8930; Fax: 1 (802) 773-6993
Email: info@tuttlepublishing.com
www.tuttlepublishing.com

Japan
Tuttle Publishing
Yaekari Building, 3rd Floor
5-4-12 Osaki, Shinagawa-ku, Tokyo 141-0032
Tel: (81) 3 5437-0171; Fax: (81) 3 5437-0755
Email: tuttle-sales@gol.com

Publisher: Eric M. Oey
Designers: Nicholas Blosch, Jeffrey Ang
Writer: S. L. Wong
Editor: Loh Ai Leen
Cartography: Violet Wong

Photographic Credits

Arthur Teng pp 2 (no. 15), 3 (nos. 5, 6, 7, 12, 13), 6 (main), 10 (main), 11 (top), 17 (top right), 24, 26 (top right), 27, 31 (middle right), 32 (top), 33 (top), 37 (bottom), 38 (bottom), 39 (top and bottom left), 40 (main and bottom), 41 (top, middle left and right, bottom), 42 (bottom left and right), 43 (middle), 48

Daniel D'Orville pp 45-47 (except p 44)

HBL Network Photo Agency Front cover (top left), back cover (bottom), pp 2 (no. 2), 3 (no. 10), 5 (main), 15 (right), 16 (middle left), 17 (bottom), 18 (top left and right, bottom), 19, 21 (bottom right), 25 (bottom right), 29 (top left and right), 31 (top right), 34 (bottom right), 35, 37 (top left), 39 (bottom right), 43 (top right)

Ingo Jezierski Front cover (top right), back cover (top right and middle), pp 2 (top left), 3 (no. 3), 11 (middle left and bottom), 16 (top, middle right, and bottom), 22-23 (main), 23 (top and bottom), 26 (bottom), 33 (middle and bottom), 34 (middle right and bottom left)

Jill Gocher Front cover (bottom), back cover (top left), pp 2 (nos. 1, 14), 3 (no. 4), 8 (top), 10 (inset), 12 (bottom left), 18 (middle), 20, 21 (top left, top right, and bottom left), 25 (middle), 26 (top left), 29 (bottom left), 31 (top left and middle left), 32 (main), 34 (top), 36, 37 (right), 42 (main), 43 (top left)

Luca Invernizzi Tettoni pp 34 (middle left)

Photobank pp 25 (top), 44

Radin Moh'd Noh Salleh pp 4 (left), 7 (right), 12 (top left, top right, bottom right), 13 (top and bottom left), 14 (top), 26 (middle left and right), 38 (main), 39 (middle left)

Ravi John Smith pp 3 (no. 8), 14 (main)

S.C. Shekar pp 8 (bottom), 13 (bottom right)

Wendy Chan pp 1, 3 (nos. 9, 11), 9, 11 (middle right), 17 (top left), 25 (bottom left), 28, 30, 31 (bottom), 43 (bottom)

Printed in Hong Kong